PLAYING AND TEACHING SAMBA

The **BEATLIFE** Book

by

Chris Preston and Stuart Hardcastle

Published by SVM Publications (UK)

www.beatlife.co.uk

You can contact the authors directly through beatlifebook@hotmail.com

THE BEATLIFE BOOK

The BeatLife Book
First Edition 2008
First Reprint 2014

Layout design by Ryan Swift
Scores by Steph Preston
Illustrations by Paul Hardcastle
BeatLife logo by Louise Flooks
Photography by Sabrina Fuller
CD Intro by Kate Brennan
Commissioning Editor - David Ledsam

Published by SVM Publications (UK), a division of:

Soar Valley Music Ltd
6 Victoria Mills
Fowke Street
Rothley
Leicestershire
LE7 7PJ
UK.

Tel: 0116 230 4926

Email: sales@soarvalleymusic.com
Web: www.soarvalleymusic.co.uk

Printed by Automedia Ltd, Loughborough.

ISBN 978-0-9525305-2-7
EAN 9780952530527

ACKNOWLEDGEMENTS

The authors would like to thank the following percussionists, workshop leaders, Samba associations and drum groups for their inspiration, motivation, tips, grooves and all round good spirit:

The BeatLife Crew (Tilo, Pepe, Louise, Mick G, Al and Mandy); Leon, Holly, Zak, Ian, Eraldo, Adriana, Sivuka and all from Meninos Do Morumbi Oldham; Dudu Tucci; Gilson Silveira; Claudio Kron; Giba Gonclaves; Lee Higgins; Jose Antonio Djalo; Roque Junior; Dan and Therese from Hands on Rhythm; Mick Hirst and Amanda Quigley; Roger Morris and the Liverpool Escola de Samba; Airto Moriera.

Special thanks goes to Gafro, Rick, Eddie, Chris and all Inner Sense members past and present for bringing the drum to so many people in the UK over numerous years. It's your fault!

The authors would also like to thank the teachers, parents and children of Windsor Community Primary, Toxteth and Gilmour Junior School, Garston for their encouragement, dedication and support throughout the BeatLife project.

A final thanks goes to Helen Flooks: your unquenchable spirit and tireless work in community arts touched so many. We all miss you dearly.

3

PREFACE

This book is primarily an educational resource for teachers and workshop leaders. However, we have also included advanced versions of the rhythms, which should be useful to drummers and musicians looking to learn more about Brazilian grooves, playing styles and instrumentation.

Neither of us are specialist Samba tutors; we are professional percussionists who have seen through leading and participating in workshops how accessible these styles are and how applicable they can be to a classroom or community environment.

The compositions presented here are our own interpretations using rhythms learnt or composed ourselves over a period of years. They are played with our own accent and should not be treated as absolute and unchangeable - the key is to understand how parts lock together to create a particular feel.

Feel and emotion is paramount in playing any form of music. Learning the names and playing techniques of the various instruments is useful but does not in itself equal freedom of expression. By the same logic, one does not become a poet simply by learning all the words in the dictionary.

Music is not a puzzle that requires solving - the beauty lies in its mystery and the emotions that it stirs in both player and listener. The reasons for those feelings are as personal as they are universal. To tap into them all you have to do is be yourself, work hard but have an open mind and ear.

Learning any instrument is an endless personal journey - every time a new technique is mastered a little mystery is solved to be replaced by a whole new spectrum of possibilities. In a band situation, the real skill comes in knowing which of those techniques or possibilities will add up to a richer whole and not to let ones ego dictate how you play. Sometimes, the simplest parts work the best and the feeling you get as an individual is magnified when you put it into a communal context with numerous clear, simple parts working together.

When entering any workshop, rehearsal or performance situation try and find that calm, open place within yourself because, ultimately, what you give is what you get.

Stuart Hardcastle & Chris Preston.

The authors would like to thank Roberto Guariglia of Contemporânea Instrumentos Musicais, São Paulo for 'instrumental' support for this project.

CONTENTS

CD CONTENTS

Ragga

Samba Batucada

Maracatu

The BeatLife Book

Playing &
Teaching
Samba

by
Stuart
Hardcastle
&
Chris
Preston

INTRODUCTION

Track 1

Drumming should be fun. It can also be educational, bring people together and provide good entertainment. In many parts of the world, drumming is a central part of the community and drummers can be found at births, weddings, deaths and celebrations of all things present or past. All around the world, drums provide the beat for people to dance to, and how you play will affect the way they move.

Drumming is very accessible. It is easy to make basic noises and under good direction those basic noises can add up to quite complicated rhythms. Large groups of people who might never have played before can create beautiful music in a short space of time.

Like anything, being a good drummer takes a lot of practise. But whether you are a performer or a teacher, the principle is the same: you have to communicate well. Drums talk to each other and the people listening, so you have to be very clear about what you and the whole band are saying.

In this book, we will look at a number of rhythms and how you can teach these (or any beats) to people of all ages. However, because it is not always possible to buy or take drums of

BeatLife performing at Liverpool Lord Mayor's Parade 2007

ALL kinds EVERYWHERE you go, we will concentrate on the instruments used in the Brazilian Samba band or 'Bateria'. These include drums both large and small, made with many different materials and played in numerous different ways so it is possible to adapt sounds from other styles of orchestra.

It is important to know that Samba refers to many different rhythms from across Brazil and that the Brazilian population in itself comes originally from many different places in Africa and Europe as well as South America. Some of the reasons for that are very bad - the Transatlantic Slave Trade and Colonisation of the New World are a big part of Brazil's history, but at the same time it is this incredible mixture of cultures and traditions that has created such beautiful music.

Part 1 explains the role, sound and playing technique of the key instruments. You can listen to an example of each of these on the CD.

Part 2 is basically a list of rhythms you can teach - explaining where they come from and what they are used for. On the CD, you can listen to individual instruments then hear them as part of the overall grooves. This is ideal for practising along to.

The material for Part 3 is presented in the order that an actual workshop could be run. We do some warm up games, and then show methods for teaching a basic groove with a beginning, middle and ending - just like a story.

Hopefully, the book will be a great resource for drummers who want to teach, teachers who want to drum and children or adults who want to do both.

THE BEATLiFE BOOK

PART ONE
The Instruments

GANZAS

Track 2

Ganzas, or Chocalhos, are cylindrical plastic, wooden or metal shakers filled with rice or seeds to create a sound like rainfall or the cymbal of a drum kit.

Ganzas are a great instrument to play when you join a band as they have a gentle sound which won't put other people off if you don't get everything right straight away. They are also good for improving flexibility and strength, which you will appreciate when you move on to some of the other drums.

When playing, it is helpful to think of the movement of the rice or seeds inside the Ganza, as these are actually what create the sound.

Ganzas are held either in the centre with one hand or at the ends using both hands. A horizontal movement to and from the body creates the basic rhythm, but by stopping abruptly at the point of extension, two lighter beats are made by the natural recoil of the wrists.

Children from Chikale School, Malawi 2007

Ganzas, like Surdos, help keep time. They are usually thrown out on the beat, but the act of stopping and recoiling before repeating will create the other beats and help make up a constant rhythm. Played correctly, with the movement to and from the body extended and the other two beats pushed together, you will create what is known as the Samba swing, like a train going over a track.

Ganzas are very easy to make. Get a couple of yoghurt pots or any other light container, fill them with a bit of rice, tape the open ends together and put whatever decorations you like on the outside.

For an audio example of the Ganza, listen to the accompanying CD, track 2.

BeatLife brass section playing Ganzas at World in Princes Park 2007

THE BEATLIFE BOOK

TAMBORIMS

Tamborims are not to be confused with tambourines. Tamborims are small, high-pitched drums which you hold up in one hand whilst beating with a stick, sometimes one that has two, three or numerous prongs to create a larger sound.

Tamborims are unique to Brazil and can be used to make long intricate patterns that float on top of the groove like a song.

There are different playing methods. The simplest way is to strike the centre and play phrases that complement the other instruments. You can vary the tone of these by keeping one finger pressed on or off the back of the skin. All drums are about vibration, and by pressing you stop the vibration creating a deader or more muffled sound compared to one that rings out.

A more complicated way, which takes some practise but is very useful for playing fast patterns, is to tilt the Tamborim so that the stick strikes it on the way up as well as the way down. When you play like this constantly, you start to hear the Samba swing, just like the Ganza.

For an audio example of the Tamborim, listen to the accompanying CD, track 3.

AGOGO BELLS

Track 4

Agogos are two or three metal bells of different sizes attached to each other by a rod. Like Surdos, and many other drums, the smaller bell will produce a higher sound. By striking the different bells with a stick one can produce melodies that complement the beats of the other instruments.

Some drum orchestras may only use a single Agogo bell. If this is the case, the player can be very free in how he or she plays, improvising and creating complex patterns that sit on top of the groove. Other groups will feature a number of bells and the players must be very disciplined, making sure that they are performing the same pattern and not clashing with each other.

Metal instruments can have a very sharp tone, so it is important to play with sensitivity.

Once you get comfortable with playing patterns on the Agogos, you can make the rhythms more interesting or challenging by pressing the bells together between the beats. You can only do this on Agogos with a flexible rod and the coordination required is similar to certain ways of playing the Caixa or Tamborim.

For an audio example of Agogo bells, listen to the accompanying CD, track 4.

Beatlife performing at Liverpool Lord Mayor's Parade 2007

THE BEATLIFE BOOK

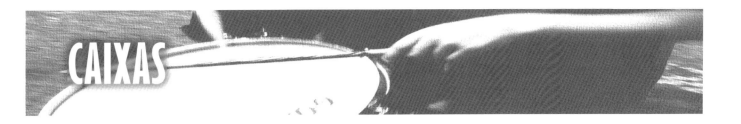

CAIXAS

Track 5

Caixa is the Brazilian equivalent of the snare commonly used with drum kits, but which has its roots in the military marching bands. In fact it was the Portuguese army bands that introduced this instrument to the early Sambas.

Snares are so named because of the gauze that runs across them, like a trap for animals. When this is tightened it creates a buzz sound, and on Brazilian Caixas this is often found on the top of the drum.

In a Samba band, the Caixas drive the rhythm forward, filling in the spaces between the Surdos to create a full sound and accenting the main beats of the groove.

The Caixa is played with two sticks, usually whilst standing up with the drum supported by a strap. The sticks can be held in two ways - match grip (which means the stick is held between thumb and index finger on both hands) or French grip where one hand is held at an angle from drum with the stick balanced in the crook of thumb and index finger. The latter way is easier when marching as you can place the snare to one side, giving your legs more mobility; the first technique is common when sitting as the posture is more balanced.

French grip

15

In either situation the main focus should be to relax as much as possible, maintaining a straight back and holding your arms at a slight angle downwards. Don't hold the sticks too tightly, or too close to either end so you have the best control possible without having to strain. Only small movements are needed.

Rhythms on Caixas are created by a combination of light notes and heavier accents, all struck near the centre of the drum skin to create a constant pattern. When you are practising these, imagine there is an invisible line above the drum and try to make sure that your sticks do not rise above it - this will help to create a feeling of balance from hand to hand. If playing for the first time, and in a group situation, the important point is simply to hit the accented notes at the right time, leaving out the lighter strokes.

Other tones that can be created are the rim shot, where the stick hits the skin and edge of the drum simultaneously to produce a very sharp sound, like an exclamation mark in grammar, and the buzz note. This is made by pressing the stick downward using the thumb to create multiple beats very close together - hence the buzz.

For an audio example of the Caixa, listen to the accompanying CD, track 5.

BeatLife workshop at Chikale School, Malawi 2001

Track 6

The Repinique is a very loud and high-pitched double headed drum, similar in some ways to a Caixa but without the snare and is traditionally used to make calls and ask questions that the rest of the band respond to or answer.

It is usually played by one of the more experienced drummers in a group and tells everyone when to start, stop or change rhythm. Sometimes it is played with one hand and one stick, sometimes with two sticks. The hand makes two distinct noises - the open tone, played by striking the skin at the edge with the fingers together then lifting; and the slap where you strike with the fingertips slightly more towards the centre to create a short snapping sound. The open tone and slap are intrinsic to playing hand drums like the Djembe and Congas, and getting clear distinction between the sounds can take some practise. The stick plays notes in the middle or at the edge to get a rim shot.

Beatlife performing at opening of Liverpool World Museum, 2004

One technique that is peculiar to the Repinique is what can be described as a triple bounce. This is where you strike the middle of the skin with the stick then pull back as it bounces so that the third bounce actually creates a click sound on the edge. In this action each beat will get shorter like the movement of a tennis ball when it bounces so that the second and third hits are closer together. The fourth beats are played by the hand making alternate open and slap notes and the overall effect recreates the Samba swing that can also be heard in the basic technique of the Ganza and the tilting of the Tamborim.

It can sometimes be easier to play the Repinique with a shortened stick to get the feel of the triple bounce more accurately. When played at a slow tempo, the bounce is replaced by two equally spaced rim shots.

For an audio example of the Repinique, listen to the accompanying CD, track 6.

SURDOS

Track 7

Bass sounds are the root on which all rhythms and melodies are 'based'.

In Brazilian Samba grooves, this sound is made by bass drums called 'Surdos'. They are the heartbeat of the band, keeping time and providing the feel for all other instruments to play on top of.

Surdos are big, barrel-shaped drums and usually have a skin on each end. They can come in a number of sizes (smaller ones have a higher tone) but ranges of three are commonly used:

Marcação - the biggest and deepest, which 'marks' the main beat. In Samba-Reggae and Batucada, this is the beats on 2 and 4.

Reposta - the next biggest, with a slightly higher tone (usually tuned a fourth above). In Samba-Reggae and Batucada, it will play the secondary beats (which is actually the 1 and 3) or 'response' to the Marcação.

Cortador - The smallest Surdo, normally playing melodies that link the beats of the other two drums (tuned a second or a third above Reposta).

To get the best sound, Surdos are played whilst standing up to let the tones ring or

BeatLife performing at Chikale School, Malawi 2007

19

resonate. This can be done with the aid of a strap, which is hooked on to the drum. A stick, called a 'beater', with a padded tip is also used as normal sticks can produce a tone that is a bit too sharp. When striking the drum, one must play hard enough to let the sound ring, but not so hard that you get a loud bang, which quickly disappears. On Marcaçãos and Repostas the other hand can be used to muffle the sound by pressing on the skin. Cortadors are usually played with two beaters.

A click sound can be added to the rhythmic groove by striking the rim with the handle of the beater, near to where it is gripped.

For an example of Surdo Reposta, listen to the accompanying CD, track 7.

THE BEATLIFE BOOK

PART TWO
Rhythms and Arrangements

UNDERSTANDING THE CD & MUSIC CHARTS

It is not necessary to read sheet music. In fact, many great percussionists do not read at all, learning instead through the essentially African oral system of say and play. However, being able to understand charts can help greatly when trying to understand a new rhythm or seeing how different grooves fit together. With drums, this is not too difficult - one must simply start slowly and be patient: notation is just a guide rather than the destination. Playing well is always the main thing.

In this book, we have superimposed traditional notation onto the much easier grid system to give people with no prior experience an idea about how music charts work. Each box on the grid represents a sixteenth note, which can be thought of as a quarter of one beat in a four beat bar, so a whole line can be counted evenly as 1 e and a 2 e and a 3 e and a 4 e and a. A mark in the box represents a note; an empty space or a musical symbol for a rest tells you there is a silence.

You can use the charts in conjunction with the CD to work out the various parts. On the CD you will hear all the instrument parts for a particular groove followed by an example of how they build up to form a rhythm. You can then listen to some breaks before hearing the whole piece as a finished composition with a beginning, middle and ending. On the CD, we have used a Ganza and cowbell to create a metronome on top of which you will hear individual parts. This is particularly useful in learning sparse or offbeat phrases. As the Ganza is the same for all rhythms used in the book, this is not included in the notation.

In teaching and learning, mnemonics can be very useful. This is when you use words to describe the beats and we have also included many examples of this on the charts. Mnemonics are also useful for naming breaks and depending on what name you give a break, you can use a visual symbol to tell people you are about to play it.

You can make different sounds on all of the drums. Please refer to the key notation box to understand which symbol relates to a particular sound or technique.

Sometimes there will be no difference in how certain instruments or breaks are played for the basic and advanced versions. 'If it ain't broke, don't fix it!'

For readers of music, it should be noted that Samba is usually felt and played in 2/4. For the sake of simplicity, however, all our scores are in 4/4.

Note Pyramid

The total value of each row is equal to the *semibreve* **at the top of the pyramid.**

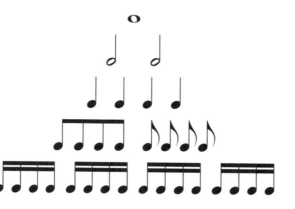

whole

half

quarter

eighth

sixteenth

Surdo

  = **open tone**

  = **rimshot**

 = **mute tone played with beater**

 = **hand on surdo**

 = **hit sticks together**

Caixa

  = **open tone**

  = **open tone accented (loud)**

 = **buzz / drag**

23

Repinique

 = open tone with stick or hand

 = rimshot

 = slap with hand

 = buzz / drag with stick

Tamborim

 = open tone

 = turn

Agogo Bells

  = top bell
= bottom bell

Ganza

 **SHAKE IT !**

24

SAMBA REGGAE

Samba Reggae comes from Bahia, in the northeast of Brazil. Its roots are in Candomblé rhythms such as Ijexa, the Samba Batucadas of Rio, Merengue from the Dominican Republic and Reggae music from Jamaica. The slow, strong pulse makes this rhythm ideal for starting to play Samba.

Historically, Reggae music has been a voice against oppression, poverty and racial or social inequality and Samba Reggae was born out of the same frustrations and injustices that many Afro-Brazilians suffer, even today.

Samba Reggae was popularised both politically and musically by groups such as Ile Aiye and Olodum: the middle break of our advanced version actually comes from an Ile Aiye workshop.

Musically it shares many of the traits of the Batucada - the Reposta and Marcação marking time while the Cortador creates melodic phrases. It also features the Caixa and Repinique strongly, but in this form the Caixa accents the upbeats in a way similar to the chop of the Reggae guitar. The Repinique often plays Clavé-based patterns.

Clavé is a Spanish word meaning 'key' and Clavés are two wooden sticks beat together to create a five beat figure which, in Cuban music especially, all other instruments must follow.

It is also worth noting that while Batucada is fast and always feels like it is pushing, Samba Reggae can be much slower and feel like you are pulling back on the beat. In fact, if Batucada is thought of as having a fast swing, then Samba Reggae has, in stark contrast, a gentle sway to it.

Protest music is a cry against injustice and unfairness. In Reggae and Samba Reggae this protest is put across in a strong but peaceful manner as if you are saying, "We are here, we have a right to be here, we shall not be moved".

RHYTHMS FOR SAMBA REGGAE - BASIC VERSION

The Surdo Reposta sets the pulse with strong beats on 1 and 3, whilst dampening with the hand on 2 and 4.

The pattern of the Surdo Marcação is a mirror image of the Reposta, playing strong beats on 2 and 4 whilst dampening on 1 and 3. When the two Surdos are played together, the foundation of the groove is formed.

The Surdo Cortador plays between the Reposta and Marcação, linking them rhythmically and melodically and creating a feel a bit like the bass guitar in Reggae. It is important to note that the Cortador dampens on 1 and 3 whilst playing open notes on 2 and 4 - this makes these the stronger beats, a feel common in both Reggae and Samba.

The basic pattern we have used for the Caixa uses the hand to echo the pulse of the Reposta and Marcação whilst playing strong upbeats with the stick. These upbeats are the main accents of the Caixa and reflect patterns you might expect to hear on the keyboard or guitar in Reggae.

In our basic version, the Repinique plays what is known as 'Son Clave'; in the advanced version this changes to 'Rumba Clave'. Both Son and Rumba are Cuban rhythms, but just like Reggae you can find elements of them in many Brazilian styles.

The Tamborim plays a one bar phrase that fills out the groove, making the overall sound richer.

The Agogo plays a variation of the Tamborim line adding a further tone and melody to the piece.

The Introduction is a call and response between the Repinique and the other instruments. This is repeated three times. Everyone then plays a bar of eighth notes that gradually get louder before entering the main groove. You can think of this section like the beginning of a story - the introduction lets us know we are about to go on a journey, so get ready.

In the Clavé Break, all the instruments play the phrase of the Repinique once. After this, the Repinique plays a short call to bring everyone back into the groove. This creates a middle section for the song - sometimes it can be tedious if the groove just continues uninterrupted without any changes or dynamics. Using breaks literally 'breaks' things up a little by adding variation to a piece of music.

The End Break allows all the instruments to finish together by playing a phrase in unison before stopping. Finishing a piece like this can be very effective, like using an exclamation mark at the end of a sentence. Even if you drift apart in the groove sometimes, it is very important to come together for the ending, like a good story that finishes happily!

BeatLife performing at Africa Oye 2007

Samba Reggae - Basic Version

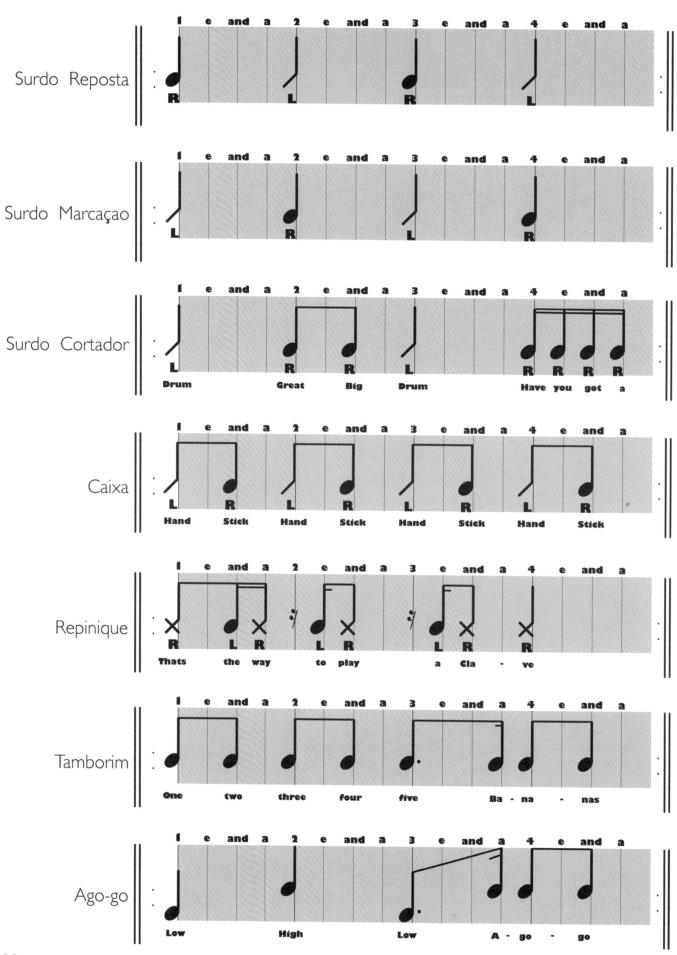

Breaks for Samba Reggae - Basic Version

INTRODUCTION

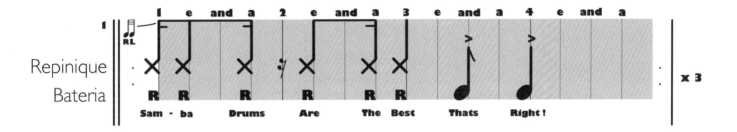

CLAVE BREAK

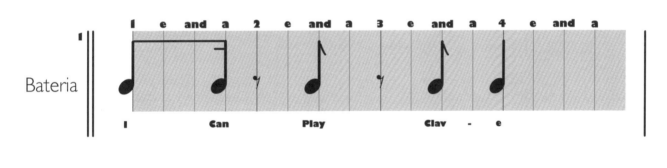

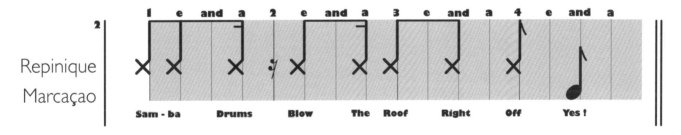

END BREAK

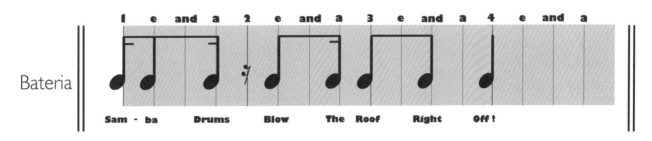

Samba Reggae - Advanced Version

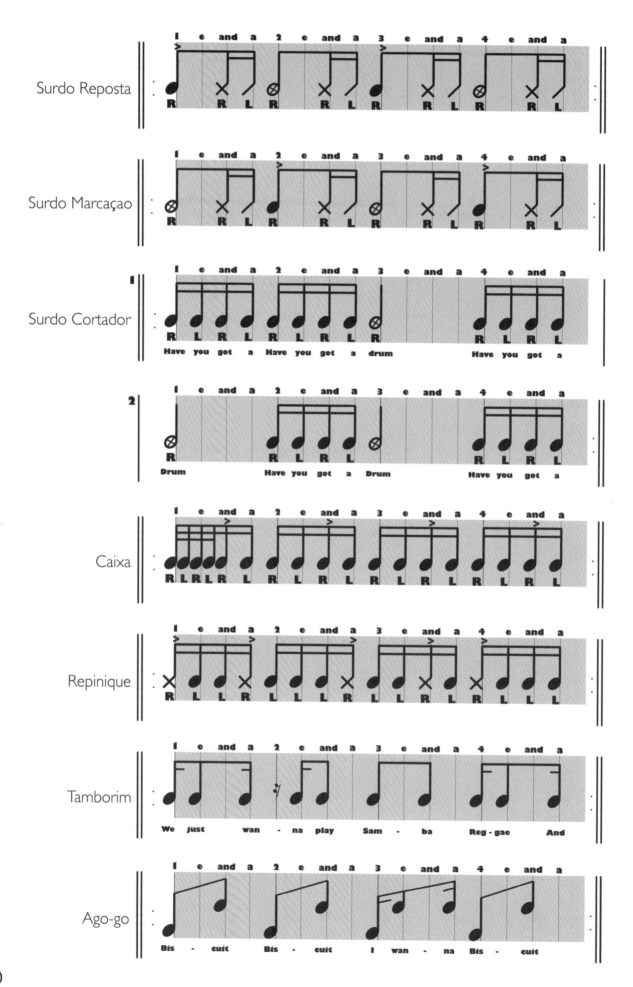

Surdo Reposta

Surdo Marcaçao

Surdo Cortador

Caixa

Repinique

Tamborim

Ago-go

Breaks for Samba Reggae - Advanced Version

INTRODUCTION

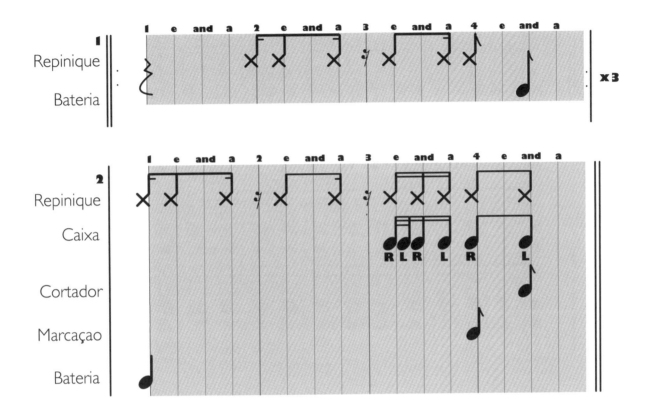

TAMBORIM BREAK

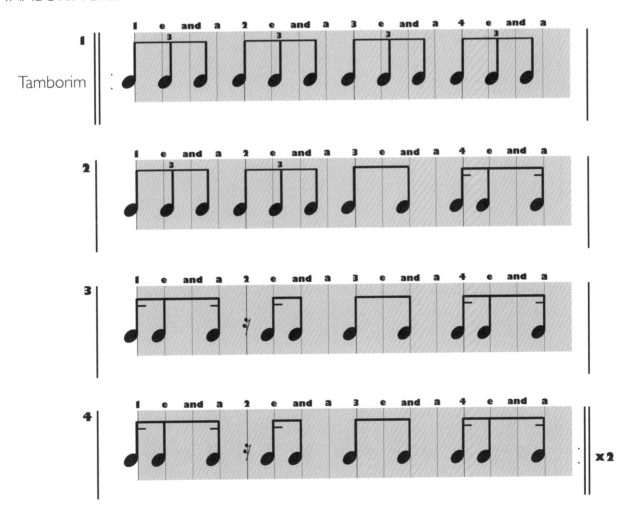

Breaks for Samba Reggae - Advanced Version

ILE AYE BREAK

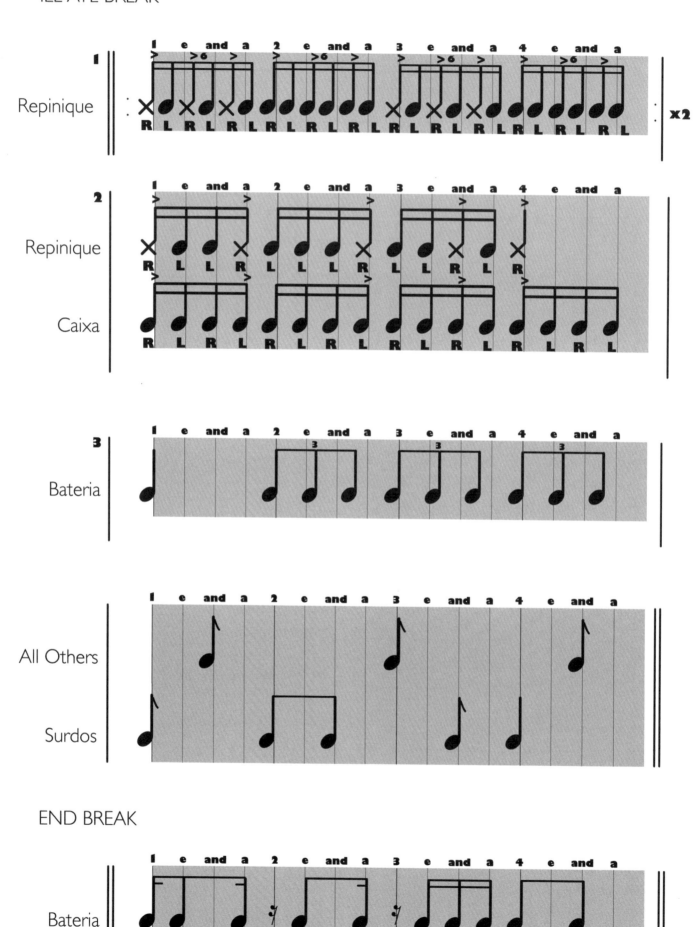

END BREAK

SAMBA FUNK

Tracks 16 to 22

Samba Funk takes the instruments of the Brazilian percussion troupe and uses them in a distinctly north American style, influenced by soul and funk artists such as the late James Brown and Brazil's own Carlinhos Brown, founder of the legendary Timbalada group. Such is the impact of this troupe that sometimes Samba Funk is actually referred to as Timbalada Funk.

Funk and rock music use the snare drum quite commonly to place a heavy emphasis on the backbeat (the beats on 2 and 4). This is supported by the other percussion instruments such as the Agogo and Tamborim, while the bass drums counterbalance this with thick beats on the one.

Funky music is quite unashamedly for dancing to and having fun. It is often slower than carnival rhythms but faster than protest music such as Samba Reggae, and it doesn't push or pull on the tempo quite as much. One of the best ways to make something funky is not to place more beats in it, but to simply leave everything out but what you need - sometimes, the simplest grooves are the best!

BeatLife performing at Africa Oye 2007
featuring Adeyinka Olushonde breakdancing

Funk - Basic Version

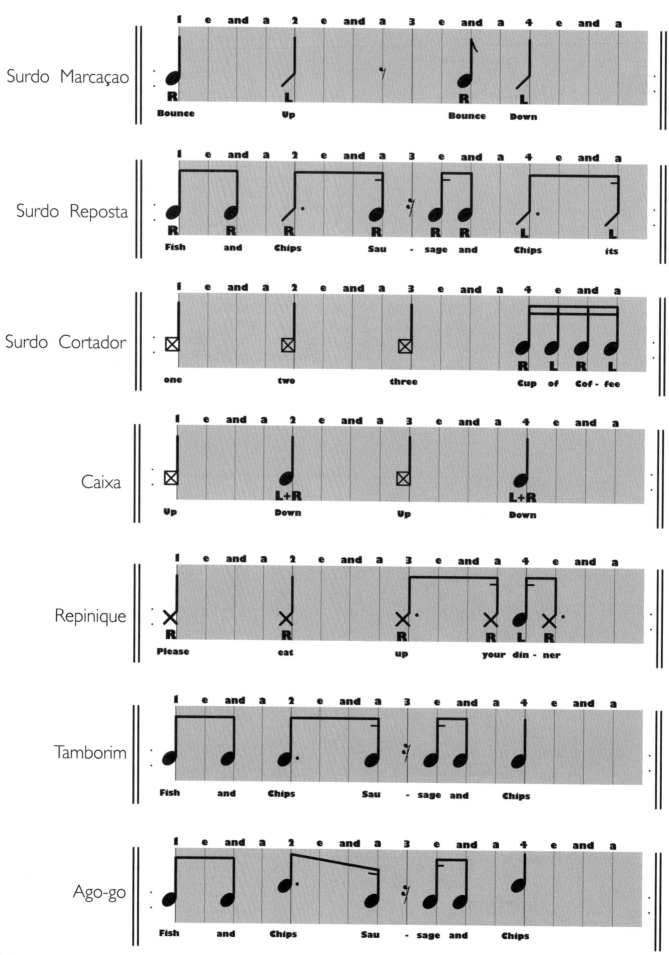

Breaks for Funk

INTRODUCTION

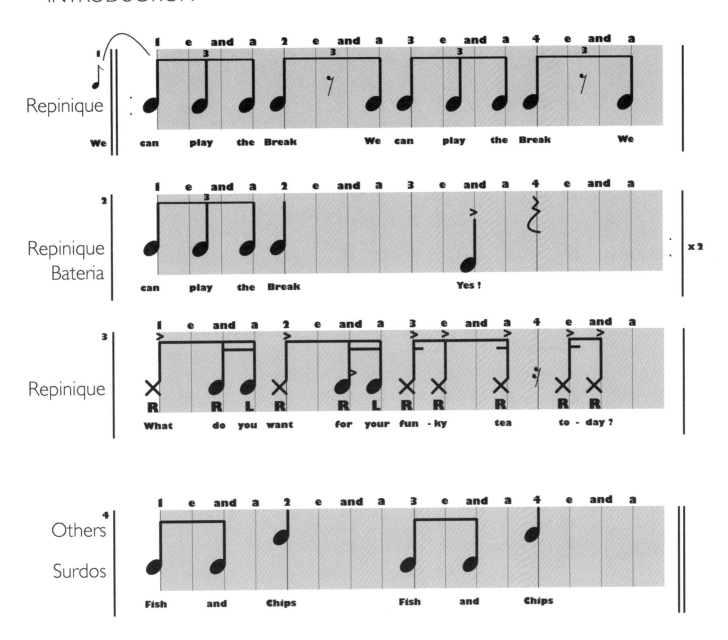

5-BEAT BREAK / END BREAK

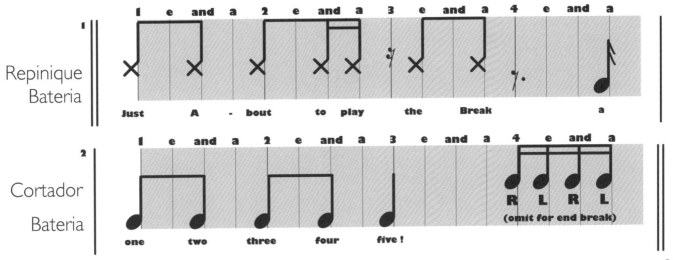

Funk - Advanced Variations

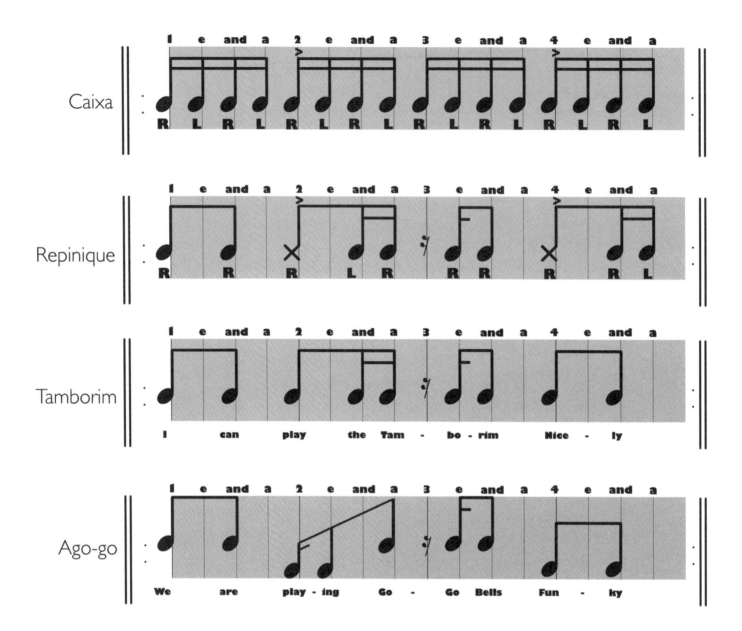

Caixa

Repinique

Tamborim

Ago-go

Tracks 23 to 29

Ijexa is a former kingdom in what is now called Nigeria. It also refers to a sacred rhythm played by the African slaves who came to Salvador, Brazil and is very important to the Candomblé rituals of that area. Candomblé is the religion of the African slaves and in it remembering one's ancestors is extremely important.

Ijexa is traditionally played on Brazilian Conga drums called Atabaques, but has been adapted in modern times to Surdos and other instruments typical to the Samba forms. When using these instruments, Ijexa is sometimes called Afoxé, but Afoxé can also mean the type of band who play Ijexa rhythms.

Ijexa features Agogo bells very highly and these play the main rhythmic pattern. The bass drums play a sparse offbeat phrase within the overall structure and the feel can be very calm compared to the up-tempo Sambas.

Beatlife performing at Africa Oye 2007

In our version, the Surdo Reposta and Cortador play the same line. In the advanced version, the Marcação plays a longer part, reflecting the fact that in older folkloric rhythms, it is sometimes the bass drums that take the solos. In modern percussion groups, the higher pitched instruments like the Repinique usually take this role.

When playing Ijexa, think of your parents, your grandparents and even their grandparents: without any of them, we would not be here.

Ijexa - Basic Version

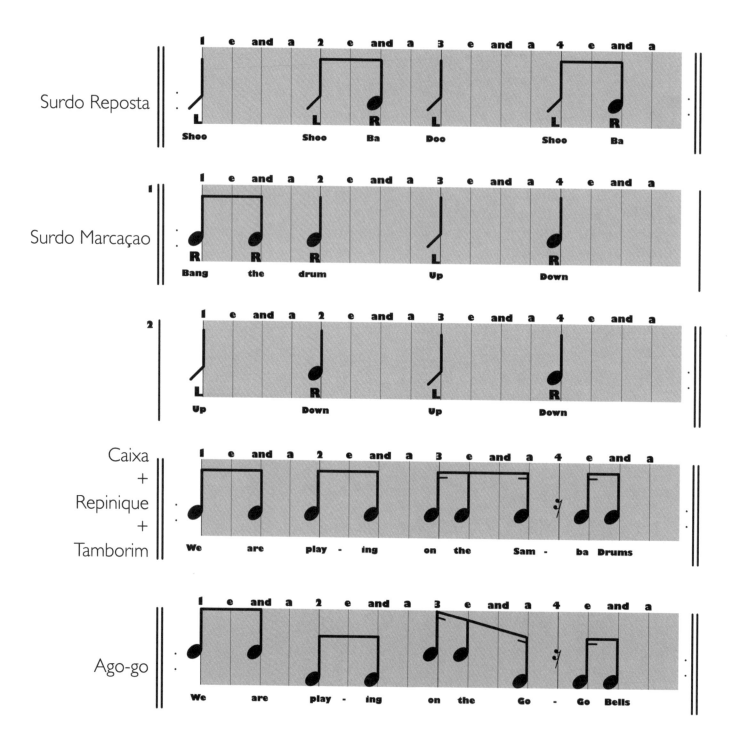

Breaks for Ijexa

INTRODUCTION

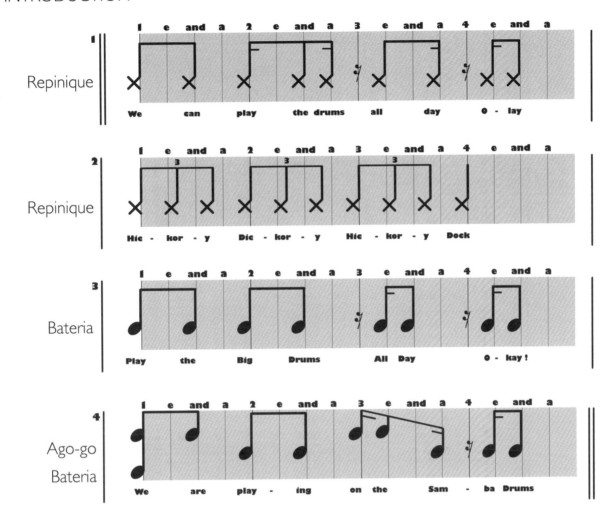

AGO - GO BREAK

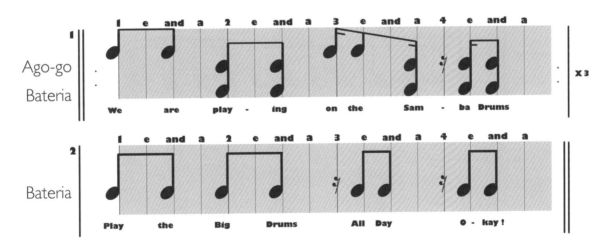

END BREAK

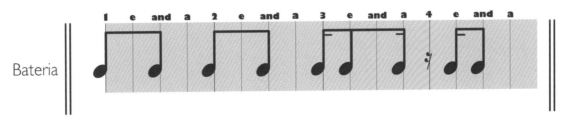

Ijexa - Advanced Variations

Surdo Reposta

Surdo Marcaçao

Caixa

Repinique

RAGGA

Tracks 30 to 36

Ragga has its roots in the reggae and dancehall music of Jamaica but has a much more modern and sometimes electronic feel. The basic rhythmic phrase, however, as emphasized by the low bass drums and snare is similar to the Baiao of north Brazil, the Calypso of Trinidad, and even the Banghra music of southern India.

In this version, all the instruments play a variation on that phrase, adding or taking away beats apart from the Cortadors, which provide the feel of an electric bass, as indeed they do in Samba Reggae.

It is important in Ragga to space the beats correctly - if this isn't achieved the overall sound will be a bit more like techno.

In our version, the middle break is really only a breakdown of the Surdos to a sparser pattern while the other instruments play through and, by doing so, feature more prominently. As a rule, dropping sections in and out can achieve a very effective sound.

Beatlife performing at Chikale School, Malawi 2007

Ragga - Basic Version

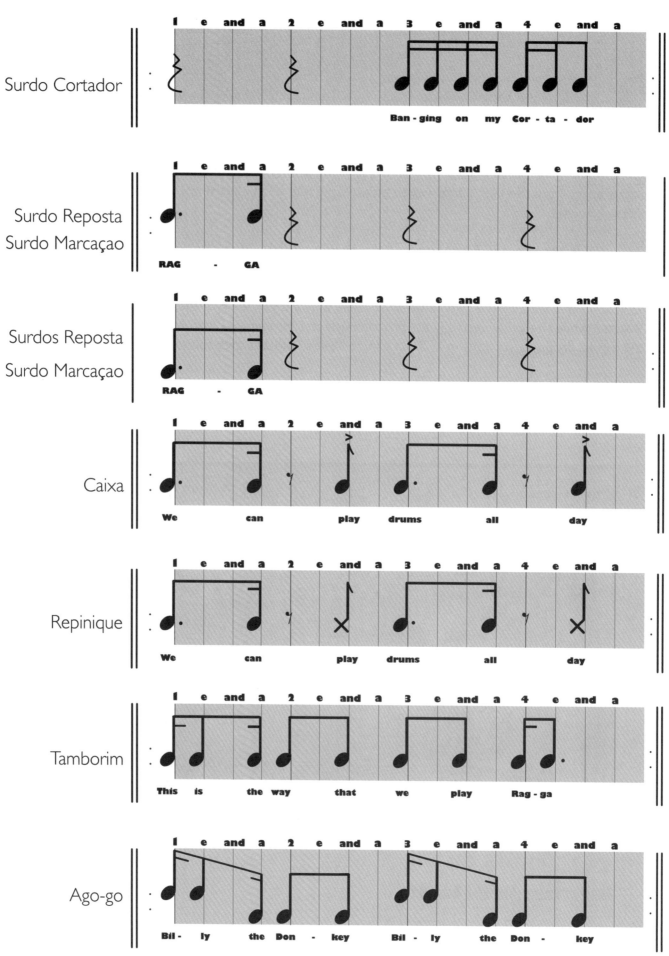

Breaks for Ragga

INTRODUCTION

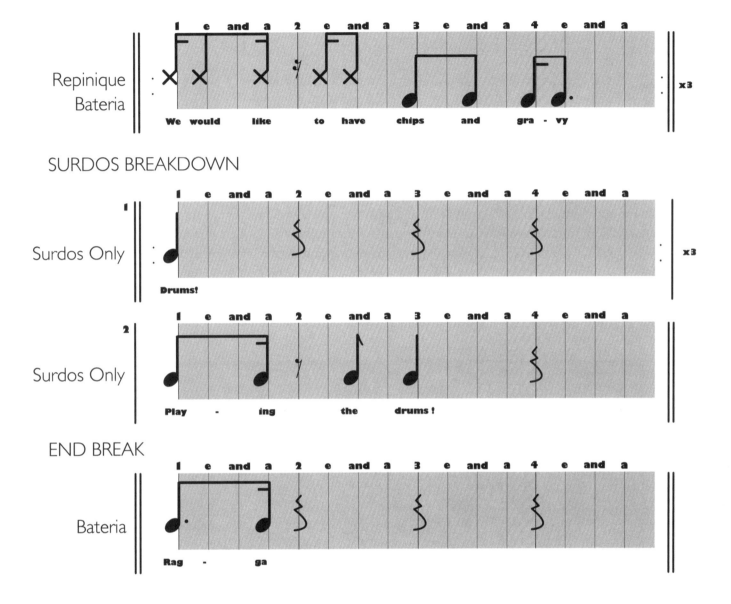

Ragga - Advanced Variations

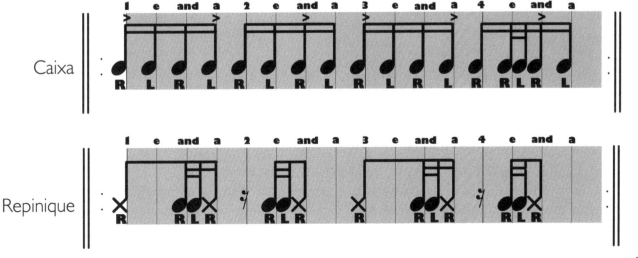

BATUCADA

Tracks 37 to 44

In English speaking countries, Samba Batucada usually refers to the rhythm played at the Rio de Janeiro Mardi Gras, the world's largest street parade. In Brazil itself Batucada simply means a gathering of percussionists and the rhythm is called the Samba de Roda or Samba de Carnaval.

Whether you call it Batucada or Samba de Roda, this rhythm is characterised by its fast frenetic nature and the large size of the orchestras (sometimes hundreds of people) who play it. It has its roots in both African traditional rhythms, such as Semba from Angola, the sacred Candomblé rituals of the African slaves and the music of the European military marching bands. At carnival time, it is accompanied by garish costumes, large intricate floats, dancers and musicians, with each group creating its own theme and vying to be crowned champions of the parade.

BeatLife performing at Liverpool Lord Mayor's Parade 2007

The Repostas and Marcação mark the downbeats creating a powerful pulse, which the rest of the band follows. The Cortadors float between these creating variations on a basic pattern that adds tension and feels like it is pushing the tempo forward. The numerous

Tamborim players will make up elaborate patterns that act like a song on top of the driving rhythm while both the Ganzas and Caixas play through the spaces to create a constant groove whilst maintaining the Samba swing. The Caixas can also put accents in certain places to influence the overall feel.

The Repiniques introduce the groove and make calls which the rest of the band answer to. In our advanced version, the Repinique actually brings the band in on beat 3, a variation very common in Rio Samba schools.

In this groove, the whole section can sometimes feel like they are running so fast, they are all about to trip over! This, however, is very important in creating the right feel: one should always try and anticipate the beat by a fraction so that the music feels as if it is pushing rather than being pulled back like you might find in Samba Reggae.

Carnival music is a celebration of life in all its forms, both big and small. It is about remembering the good times and overcoming the bad times; it is about giving thanks for our existence and sharing that with other people, coming together for one big party.

Beatlife performing in Malawi, 2007

Samba Batucada - Basic Version

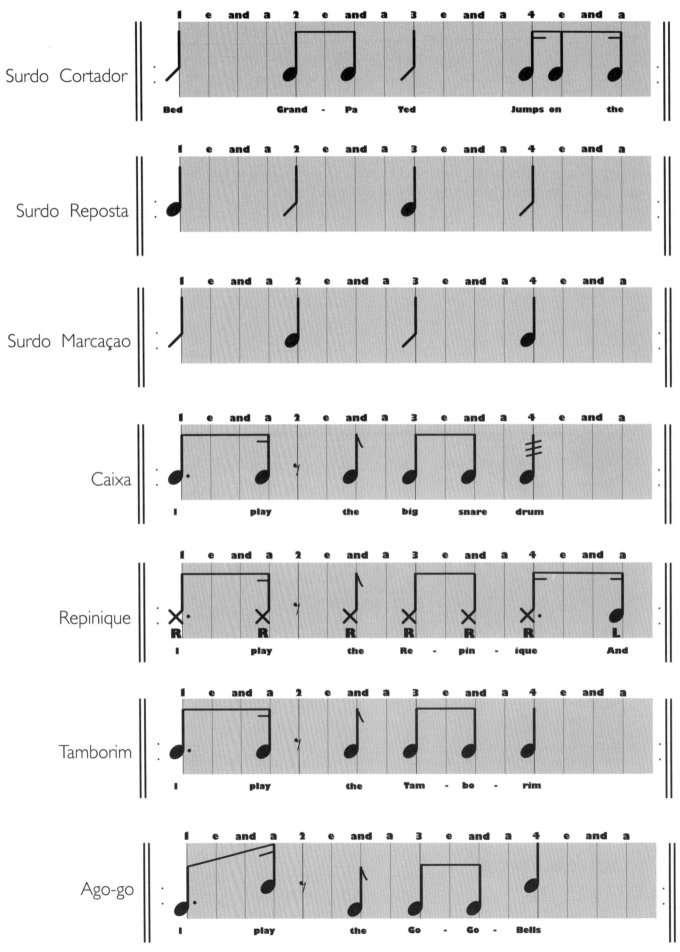

Breaks for Samba Batucada - Basic Version

INTRODUCTION

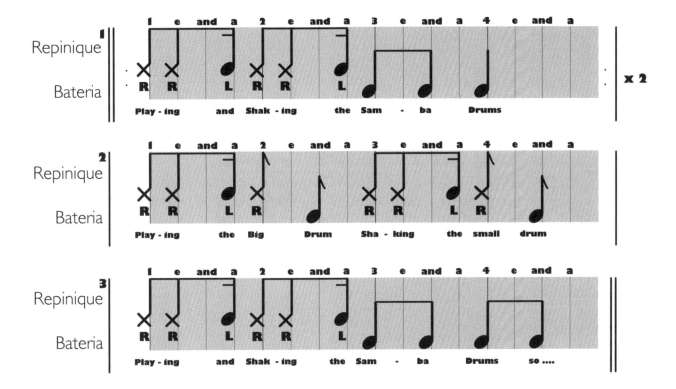

TAMBORIM BREAK

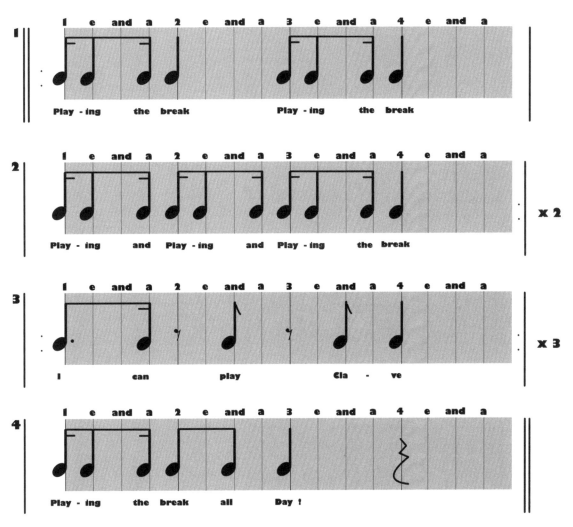

Breaks for Samba Batucada - Basic Version

THUMB BREAK

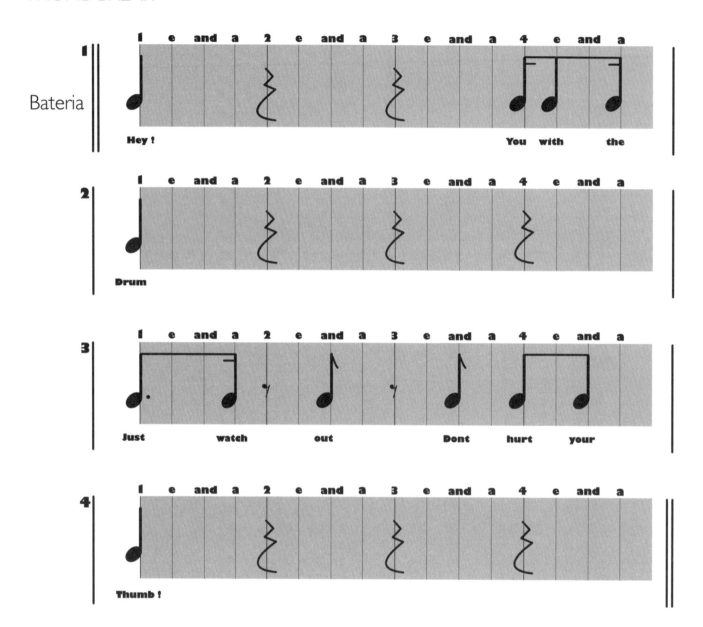

END BREAK

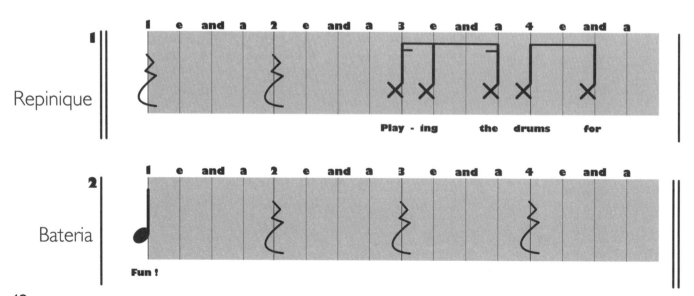

Samba Batucada - Advanced Variations

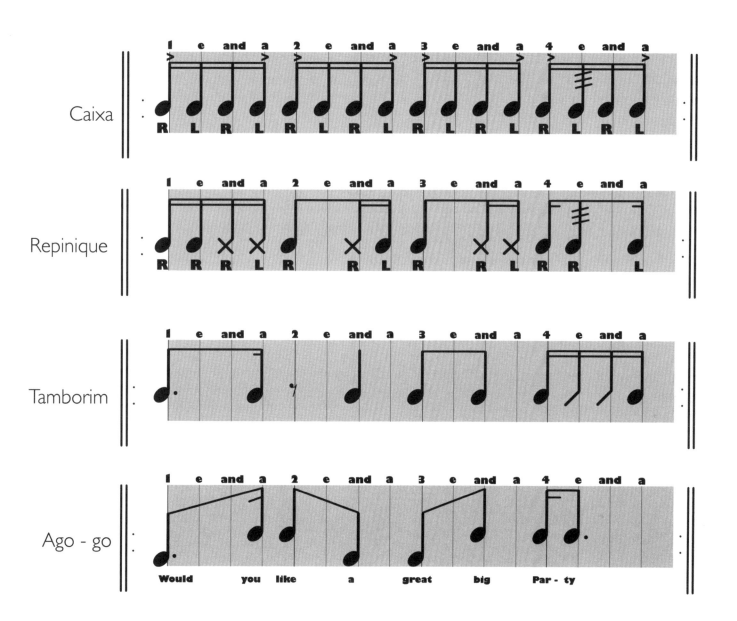

Caixa

Repinique

Tamborim

Ago - go

Would you like a great big Par - ty

Breaks for Samba Batucada - Advanced Variations

INTRODUCTION

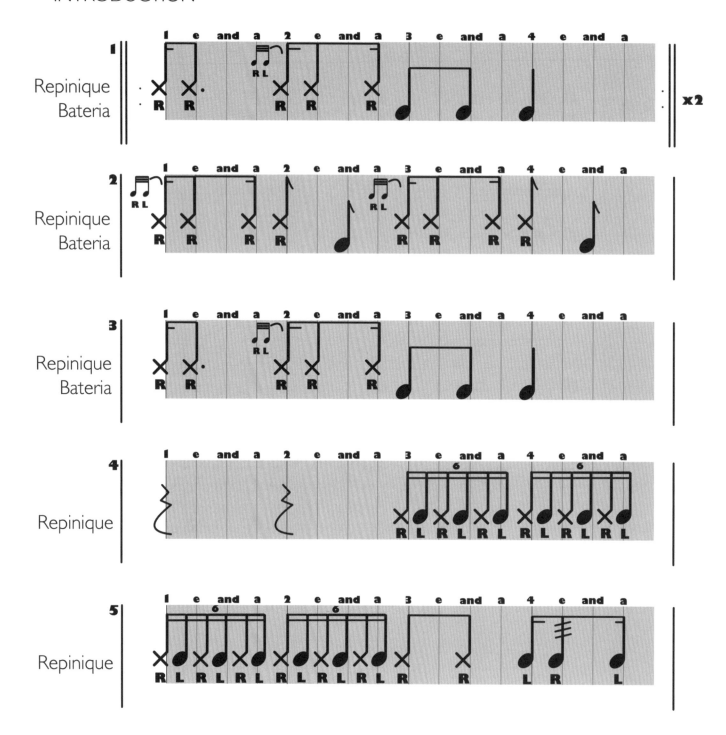

INTRODUCTION CONT.

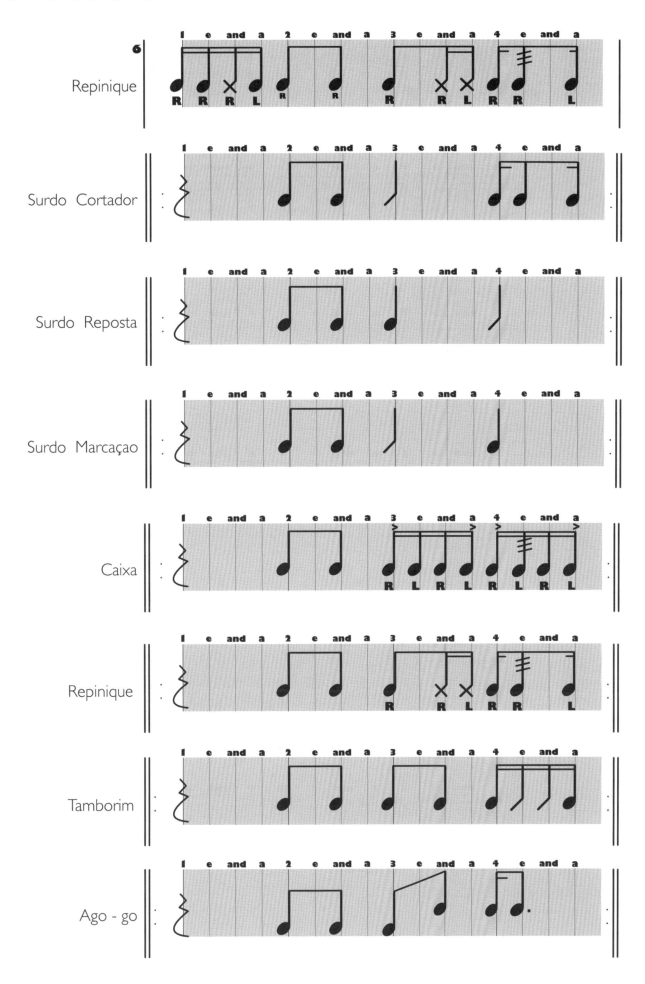

Breaks for Samba Batucada - Advanced Variations

TAMBORIM BREAK

Tamborim

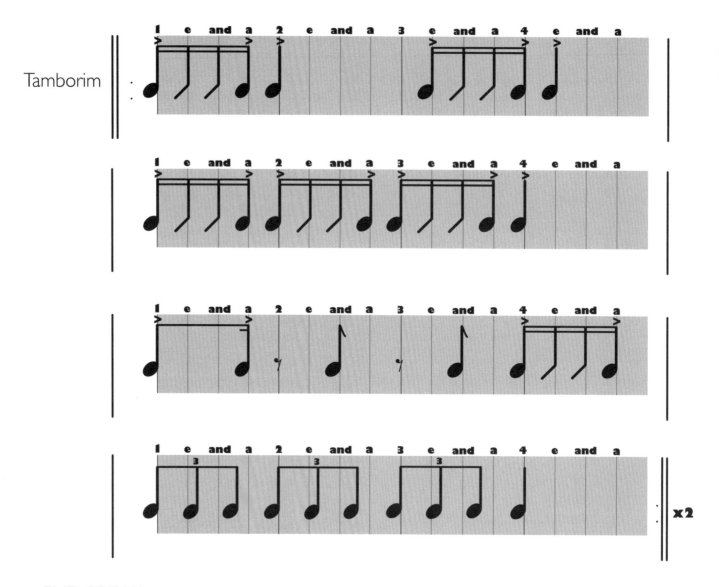

END BREAK

Repinique

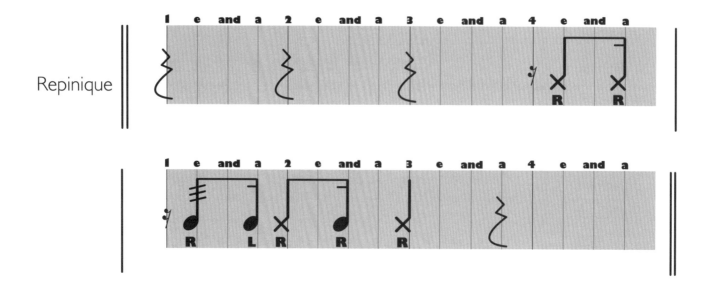

MARACATU

Tracks 45 - 51

Maracatu originates in Recife in the north of Brazil. It has its roots in rhythms such as Congado, processional forms that celebrated the crowning of African kings and is strongly linked to the slaves who came from the Congo.

Traditionally, Maracatu is played with a large bell called a Gongue, a wooden frame snare drum (Caixa de Guerra) and a rope tuned wooden bass drum (Alfaia). However you can also use an Agogo bell, Caixa and Surdo to recreate the sound and in this arrangement we have also included parts for the Tamborims and Repinique.

The bell part is extremely important in Maracatu as its rhythmic phrase marks the downbeat very strongly while the bass and snare both play quite syncopated phrases. Maracatu swings in a similar way to Samba Batucada, but with a lazier feel and one has a feeling of slowing down before catching up on the 1 of the bar again. The contrast of the bell and bass also gives this music quite a funky feel; similar to some grooves you might expect to hear in modern R&B.

In our version, all the Surdos play the same part and the middle break only lasts half a bar so that when you come back into the groove, the rhythm has turned around and beat 3 is now beat 1.

Maracatu - Basic Version

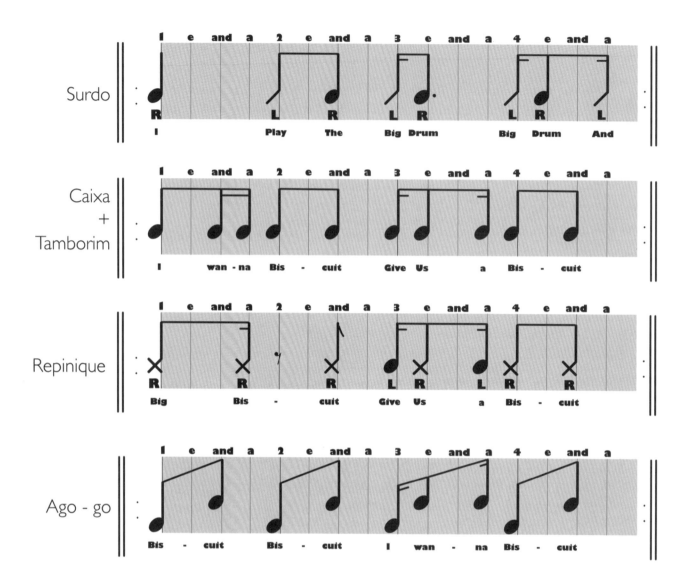

Maracatu - Advanced Variations

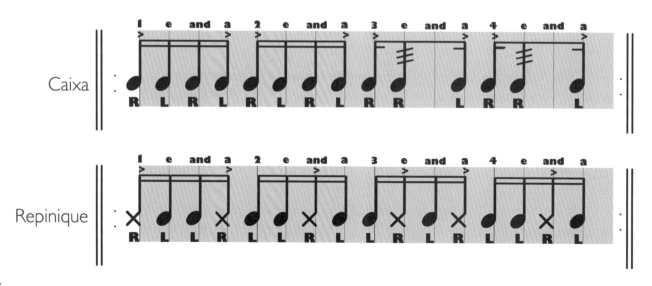

Breaks for Maracatu - Basic Version

INTRODUCTION

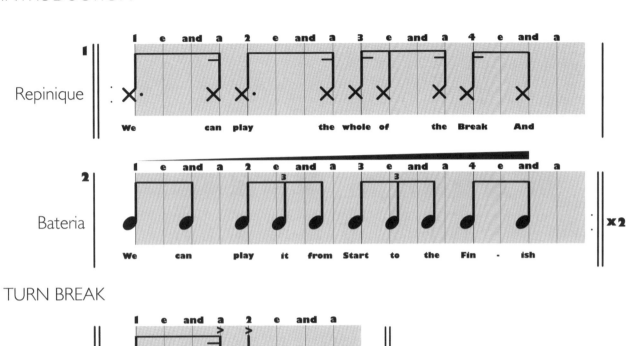

TURN BREAK

END BREAK

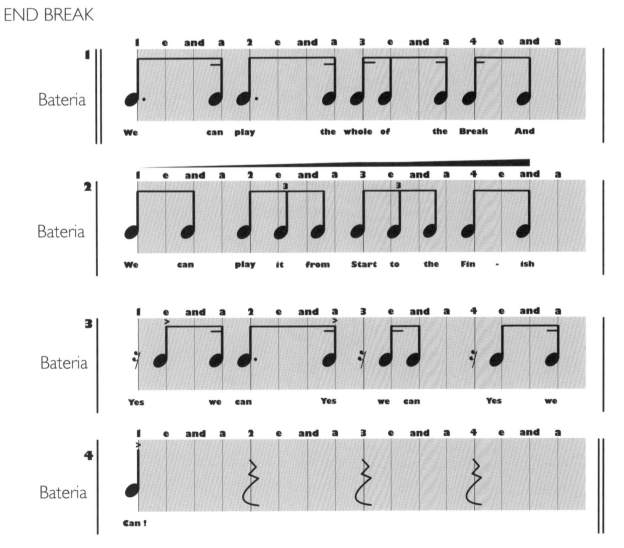

THE BEATLIFE BOOK

PART THREE

Delivering a workshop

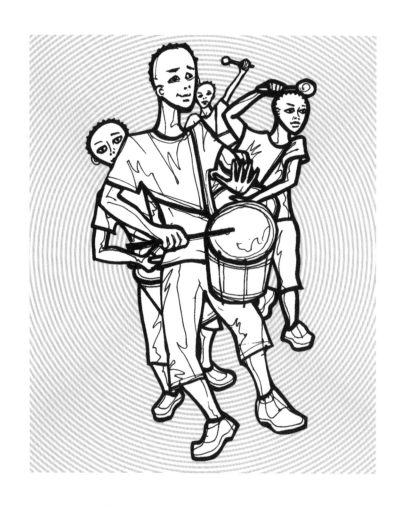

WARM UPS

Drumming can be a very physical activity. You might find yourself playing very fast patterns or standing up and marching with a large drum for a long time. For these reasons and others, you should treat drumming like any other sport and warm up and down properly so that you are relaxed and prepared in both mind and body.

If you are leading a workshop, especially if it is with a new group who might not know you or even each other, warm up games and exercises are a great way of breaking the ice - and establishing for yourself what level to pitch the session at. All kinds of game can be used, but a few guidelines might help in the delivery - keep it SHORT, SNAPPY and SIMPLE - and make sure it relates to the overall theme: RHYTHM.

On the following pages you will find a few games that can be incorporated into workshops. There are endless possibilities and you should not be frightened to make up new things. Be brave, be silly, but just make sure your delivery is CONFIDENT and CLEAR. Over a series of classes, all games and ideas can be developed, becoming more complicated as students get familiar with the routines.

A good energetic warm up might leave people a little out of breath and this can be a good time to sit down and learn about how the drums are actually played.

THE BEATLIFE Book

GAME 1 - 'MY NAME IS ...'

When a new group arrives, a good way of starting is to make a circle with everybody standing up. Wait till everyone is calm and settled then introduce yourself and the kind of activities that will be looked at, establishing an order for the session.

The first game is simply a chance for participants to introduce themselves to you. Using a count of 4, get everyone to clap or stamp on beats 1, 2 and 3 whilst leaving a silence on 4 itself. In time with the pulse everyone chants "my-name-is", then one person at a time (going either clockwise or anti-clockwise) calls out his or her name on the silent beat.

If you create the rhythm by stomping from foot to foot on beats 1 and 2, then clapping on 3, pupils might notice that this is the groove to 'We Will Rock You'.

This is a great opportunity to make eye contact and engage with each person, even if it is just for a second. From this, you can start to work out what sort of characters you have in the class and how the group dynamic could develop. Some people will be confident, some quiet - some might just be plain silly! It all helps, however, when starting to think about the distribution of drums later on - you might not want to put the loudest people on the largest drums straight away.

In a large group, you probably will not remember all names straight away and it will be the louder ones that stick in your head, but it is good practise to remember the quietest ones too, so you can give encouragement later. Over successive weeks, this is a great way of learning ALL names and stimulates confidence - tell pupils to be PROUD of their name and say it LOUD - although they don't need to shout!

One interesting variation is to ask students to replace their real name with a stage name or alias. This can fire the imagination and lead to some very interesting replies.

GAME 2 - FOLLOW THE LEADER

This game is great for loosening minds and limbs and really helps to establish the ability range in a group.

Start by explaining how drummers might count to a 4/4 beat - 1, 2, 3, 4 and repeat. Next show how to do this at twice the speed by chanting "1 and 2 and 3 and 4" then do it at twice the speed again so the count is "1e and a 2 e and a 3 e and a 4". Finally, show how rhythmic phrases are created by simply leaving gaps (for example 1 and 2, 3 e and a 4). It might not make sense straight away but in context, it soon becomes clear.

In the game itself, stamp, clap, shake or beat on the body a one bar rhythm whilst chanting the count. Students then copy both the movement and chant. As the exercise progresses, try replacing numbers with syllables or phrases to describe the beat - for instance "1 and 2, 3 e and a 4" can become "great big drum, have you got a drum" - very similar to our basic version for the Cortador in Samba Reggae. As a general rule, the sillier you make the phrases, the more memorable they will be and depending on the character of the group you can make both movement and rhythm as energetic, silly or complicated as you want.

Over a course of weeks, this can be developed to quite an advanced level, perhaps making the phrases last two, three or even four bars.

GAME 3 - PASS THE PULSE

This game develops teamwork and listening abilities.

Set up a strong pulse and get participants to clap the beats one by one around the circle. As the group becomes more confident vary the tempo, experimenting with very fast and very slow pulses.

As a development, you can substitute a basic pulse with actual rhythmic phrases. Again, participants clap only one beat as the rhythm moves around the circle, so that the entire part is created through group cooperation and focus.

GAME 4 - PASS THE BEAT

In this game we shift from a circle to a square and each side is given a number from 1 to 4. Each number is then given an action (stamp, clap, maybe even whoop!).

Using a count of 4, the sides perform the action on their corresponding number, creating a simple pulse, which is characterised by the different noises on each beat. Once the pulse is established, you can make it more interesting and dynamic by speeding up, slowing down, getting quieter then louder or even swapping who does what.

A great development of this is to change from a square to a triangle so that you create a 3/4 or waltz feel. Over a period of time you can even look at odd time meters such as 5/4 and 7/4.

GAME 5 - UPBEATS AND DOWNBEATS

In this exercise the class are divided into pairs. Person A holds their arms out so one is directly above the other with their palms facing each other. Person B holds their arms out horizontally with their palms facing each other.

Person A will start to clap a basic pulse bringing their arms up and down vertically. The movement will look something like the snapping jaws of a crocodile but what they are actually doing is creating what is known as the downbeat.

Person B claps horizontally between these beats both physically and in respect to the tempo: they are creating the upbeat of the rhythm.

Start this exercise slowly, letting pairs develop at their own speed, but get them to try and focus as a team to make the overall pulse progressively quicker. After a while, reverse the roles so that person B will provide the downbeat.

This is very similar to the technique used in Flamenco clapping and is an excellent way of improving a student's ability to play offbeat patterns.

THE BEATLIFE BOOK

DEMONSTRATING THE INSTRUMENTS

It can be very inspiring for pupils to see you actually playing the instruments. Not only does it put the session in context, but it also helps demonstrate standards that can be achieved. This is not simply showing off - if you want people to celebrate their own accomplishments, you should not shy away from doing the same.

Of course, it is not always possible to play everything at the highest level and you can always make the point of demonstrating the sound of an instrument but clarifying that you are NOT AN EXPERT. However, it is useful to include one drum you are good on and you should always aim for technical proficiency on anything you intend to teach.

THE BEATLIFE BOOK

In a lesson, take time to explain each one individually including how it is made, what type of sound it makes, how it is played and what its function is within the band. It can be good to get a class to repeat the names of drums back to you - both in English and where applicable the mother tongue.

Over several weeks, you can gradually introduce even more instruments or show more advanced techniques for the ones you already have.

WRIST EXERCISES

Wrist exercises are very important in any situation where you are intending to drum for a period of time, or on an ongoing basis. They promote good technique and minimise the risk of sustaining or aggravating injuries such as tendonitis or tennis elbow.

The most relevant time to do these is just before students actually play the drums. Like the warm ups, keep all exercises SHORT and clearly explained. The first two in this section are for limbering up and stretching, the last two help with independence from hand to hand.

THE BEATLIFE Book

Exercise 1

Bring hands up to chest and let them flop at the wrist (so that the class looks like a field of rabbits). Slowly move them up and down from the wrist as if paddling in the air, making sure there is no movement or tension in the upper arms and that breathing is controlled. Gradually speed up the action without becoming stiff.

Exercise 2

Fully extend one arm and grab the fingers with other hand. Slowly pull back until you feel the tendons stretching then release and repeat about five times. Afterwards swap and repeat the whole exercise with the other arm.

Exercise 3

Close eyes and raise hands to the level of chest. Slowly draw an imaginary triangle with one hand whilst the other makes a square.

Exercise 4

Put one finger on nose and one finger on earlobe so that arms are crossed. Without poking yourself or anybody else, swap round so that the other finger is on nose or earlobe, but arms are still crossed!

PUTTING IT ON TO DRUMS

The point where a lot of workshops can break down is at the time when people actually get on to drums, especially young children. They WANT to play, they WANT to make noise, but if it isn't controlled, everyone will leave with a headache.

This can happen when a teacher isn't methodical about placing pupils on certain drums or attempts to show a polyrhythmic piece straight away by looking at individual sections one by one. To do that, you have to really trust in the behaviour and patience of a class which, if warm ups were successful, can't wait to get started.

In this scenario, there can be too much pressure on the people you are focussing on to get it right straight away while others are frustrated by having to keep quiet. A less desirable answer is to take only one kind of drum and teach everyone the same line, but this doesn't really demonstrate the essence of a percussion orchestra - simple parts locking together to create a rich sound.

One answer is to go back to methods used in warm ups and use the intrinsically African system of call and response. Try and divide students equally among the drums - if there are 20 pupils, for instance, you could place 4 on Agogos, 4 on Ganza, 4 on Tamborim, 4 on Caixa and 4 on Surdo. Use chairs or benches to create a semi circle with everyone sitting in front of their respective instrument, with Surdos and Caixas simply resting on the floor, chairs or ideally stands. This is not how you might perform but it saves having to worry about straps straight away, which can consume a lot of time.

Put yourself on a Repinique or another suitable lead instrument and do a one-bar phrase that the class plays back to you.

Just like the exercises, start simple and gradually make the patterns more complicated. Count or chant the phrases and encourage students to do the same back. "If you can say it, you can play it!" Within the call and response, play the figures that you intend to use in the actual rhythm you will be doing. In this manner, all the class will start to learn all the lines without consciously realising it.

After a while, stop then SLOWLY and METHODICALLY swap groups from one instrument section to the next (for instance Agogos move to Ganzas, Ganzas to Surdos). This really avoids confusion about who plays what, and you can reinforce this by clearly explaining how, after a number of rotations, EVERYBODY will have played EVERYTHING.

During these rotations, you can either continue with the call and response format or introduce other elements that you might use as part of the eventual piece - intros, outros, unison breaks and rumbles. Calls where the Repinique plays one line and the class respond with a different phrase can be a great variation to just listening and copying, but the really important thing is that everything you teach at this stage is learnt by everyone at the same time.

Beatlife workshop at Windsor Community Primary

THE RUMBLE

A 'rumble' is where everyone plays as fast as possible to create a sound a bit like a continuous roll of thunder. Directed well, it can be an excellent way of learning about dynamics and tonal qualities. When it is bad, though, it can be a truly horrible noise!

Bands usually play rumbles as an introduction, like saying "here we are", or more commonly at the end of a song or performance. The key point is that everyone stops at the same time, so that one goes from a large noise to total silence in a split second.

BeatLife performing at Lake of Stars Festival, Malawi 2007

However, during a rumble, the director can do lots of interesting things. By raising your arms you can get people to play even louder; by lowering them people will play quiet and you can switch from one to the other at a fast or slow pace, creating an effect like waves on a beach. You can point at one section at a time and encourage them to play either above or below the general level of sound so you get really different sounds coming through. If you are feeling brave, get one of the students to lead it for you - this is great at building confidence.

Rumbles can be a great way of starting or stopping a phase in the lesson, so that everyone knows that a rotation is coming up and something new will be learnt or played.

Once the whole class has played every instrument, and learnt every part in unison that you intend to use, plus intro, breaks and outro, it is time to put everything together in a performance piece. At this stage, you have made the various bits of the jigsaw and the only thing left is to assemble it.

This is the point where rotation might be counter productive, so place people where you think they will do the best jobs, the warm ups both on and off the drums will hopefully have given a good idea of where this is. Explain that every instrument is vital to the overall sound and that students need to think of themselves as a team - no one person is more important than another.

Start one section off at a time - this shouldn't take too long given that the phrases have already been learnt, but it may take a few moments to settle down and feel solid. Don't expect perfection straight away - bring all the instruments in and let the groove form and play itself for a bit.

Once you are happy, stop, and bring everyone in together on a count of 4. Repeat this at both faster and slower tempos to reinforce learning then start to include intros, breaks and outros. Approach the piece like a story with different chapters. How many chapters you write will depend on the length of time you have and the collective ability of the group - just make sure the tale has a BEGINNING, a MIDDLE and an ENDING.

CONCLUSION

A good workshop flows at a steady pace - not too slow, but not too hurried either and is well balanced between exercises, demonstrations and playing. It is very important to have all the different sections in your head (just like a teachers lesson plan) and have a good sense of the time to spend on each. Dividing the session up is really important, especially with younger children, who can do amazing things, but are liable to grow bored or tired if you simply repeat the same thing over and over again. Think about it all in five, ten or fifteen minute blocks and try to keep a consistent rhythm to your delivery - your own energy and enthusiasm is the most essential ingredient.

If you have a number of sessions, or will be teaching on an indefinite basis, establishing a routine so that pupils feel familiar can be really beneficial. Revisit games and exercises each week, but try to develop them so that pupils see the progression in what you are doing. Over time, more and more of the lesson will actually be on the drums but do this gradually - as well as learning techniques and rhythms, students also have to develop CONCENTRATION and STAMINA.

Arranging a performance to show what you have learnt is great for building confidence and enthusiasm - it puts everything into context. Make it more interesting by adding bits of choreography to the piece, even if it is just stepping from side to side, and constantly stress the importance of enjoying the activity and SMILING. When you smile, you are relaxed, when you are relaxed you play better and when you play well AND smile, everybody enjoys watching or taking part!

THE BEATLiFE BOOK

PART FOUR
Appendices

All the workshop games and 'call and response' ideas are applicable from age 4-5 upwards as they only rely on a child's ability to count to 4 and recognise simple phrases and movements.

Through taking part in these activities, however, they will learn about many essential components in playing music - pulse, tempo, dynamics, coordination, repetition, melody, tone and timbre.

The basic rhythms are applicable from age 7-8 upwards and teach structure, differentiation and polyrhythm in addition to what is learnt through warm ups.

The advanced rhythms require some degree of skill and experience but are applicable up to university level as a field of study for any aspiring musician.

The BeatLife team with teachers and governors from Chikale School, Nkharta Bay, Malawi.
BeatLife visited the school to set up links with children in Liverpool whilst performing at the Lake of Stars festival in 2007.

GLOSSARY

(of Brazilian names not found in Contents Table)

ALFAIA - Wooden bass drum used in MARACATU

AFOXÊ - Rhythm or band that play the rhythm based on IJEXA

ATABAQUE - Brazilian Conga drum used in CANDOMBLÉ

BAHIA - State in NE Brazil from which SAMBA REGGAE originates

BAIAO - Rhythm from NE Brazil, similar to RAGGA

BATERIA - A percussion band, usually a group playing BATUCADA

CANDOMBLÉ - Music and Religion of the African slave descendants

CAIXA DE GUERRA - snare drum used in MARACATU

CHOCALHO - another name for a GANZA

CONGADO - Processional dance from which MARACATU comes

CORTADOR - In a set of three, the smallest SURDO

GONGUE - Large bell used in MARACATU

ILE AIYE - Important Brazilian band, forefathers of SAMBA REGGAE

MARCAÇÃO - The largest SURDO

OLODUM - Famous Brazilian band, innovators of SAMBA REGGAE

RECIFE - Brazilian city, home of MARACATU

REPOSTA - The second largest SURDO

RIO DE JANEIRO - Famous Brazilian city, home of SAMBA BATUCADA

SALVADOR - City in Bahia with strong links to the roots of IJEXA

SAMBA DE CARNAVAL - Another name for SAMBA BATUCADA

SAMBA DE RODA - Another name for SAMBA BATUCADA

TIMBALADA - Famous Brazilian band, innovators of SAMBA FUNK

Selected Discography

Dudu Tucci 'Obatimale' (WeltWunder, 4-013822-010429)

Various 'The Rough Guide to Brazil: Bahia' (World Music Network, 6-05633-11353-5)

Timbalada 'Tribal Bahia' (Universal Music, 6-02498-07432-9)

Unknown 'Batucada Brasileira' (DiscMedi Blau, 8-424295-024855)

Selected Bibliography

Ed Uribe 'The Essence of Brazilian Percussion and Drumset' (Warner Bros, 0-7692-2024)

Birger Sulsbruck 'Latin American Percussion - Rhythms and Rhythm Instruments from Cuba and Brazil' (Den Rytmiske Aftenskoles Forlag, 87-87970-08-2)

Peter Fryer 'Rhythms of Resistance - African Musical Heritage in Brazil' (Pluto Press, 9-780745-307312)

Claus Schreiner 'Musica Brasileira - A History of Popular Music and the People of Brazil' (Marion Boyars, 0-7145-3066-2)

Selected DVDs / Videos

Cassio Duarte 'Introduction to Brazilian Percussion' (Warner Bros, 0-7579-1572-8)

Airto Moreira 'Listen and Play' (DCI Music Video, 0-29156-06922)

Jean Christophe Jacquin 'In the Heart of Rios Baterias' (Le Salon De Musique, 3-553301-100520)

Please note, there is a wealth of material available on the music and history of Brazil and the African Diaspora, and the above recommendations represent only a small part of this.

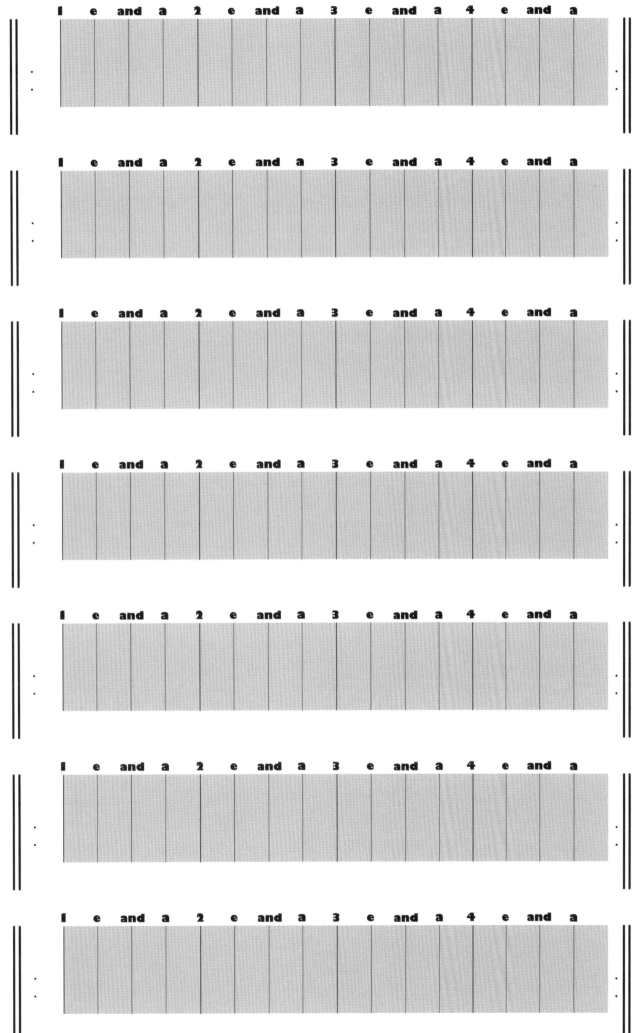

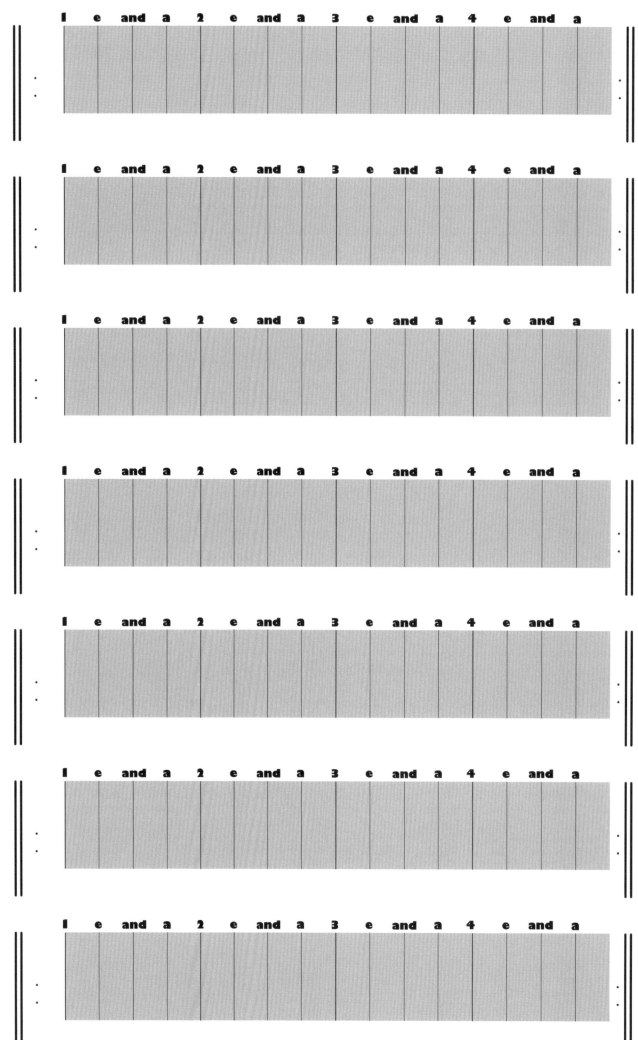

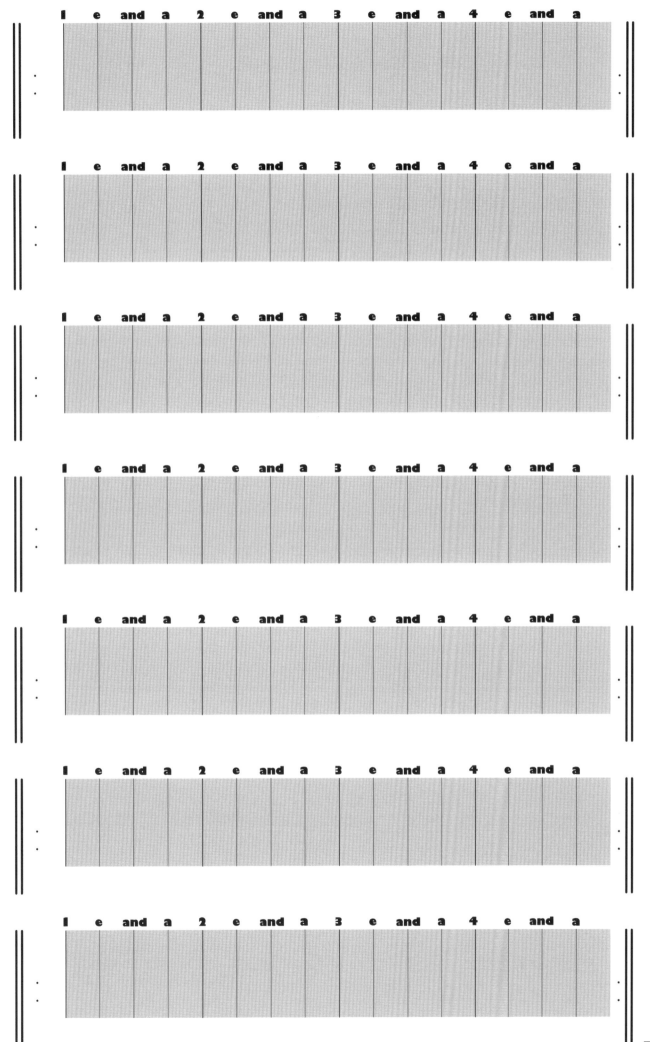

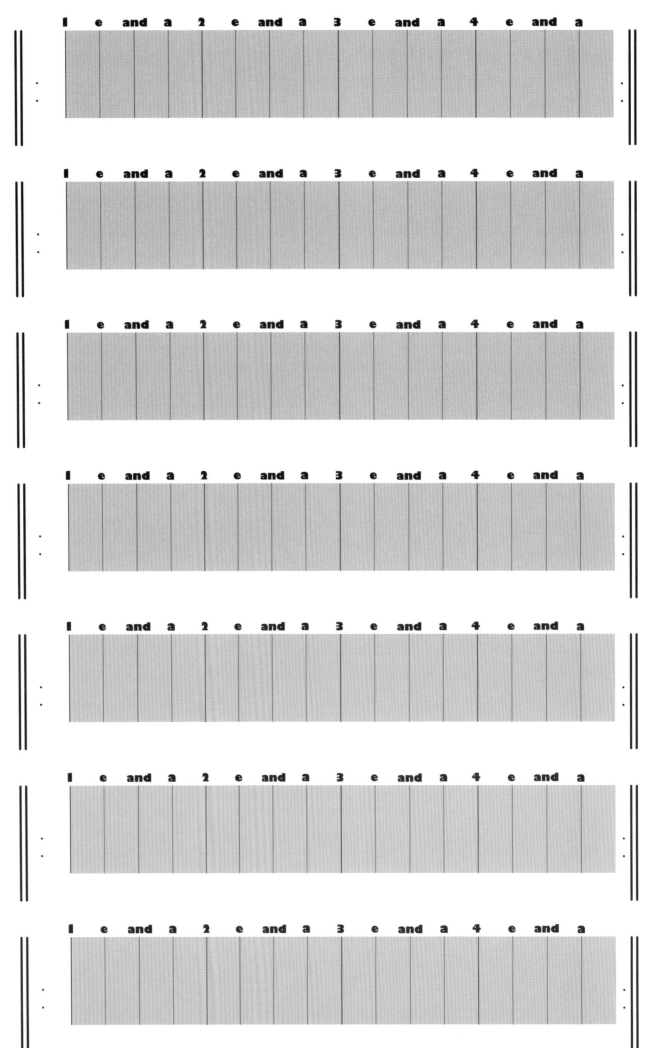

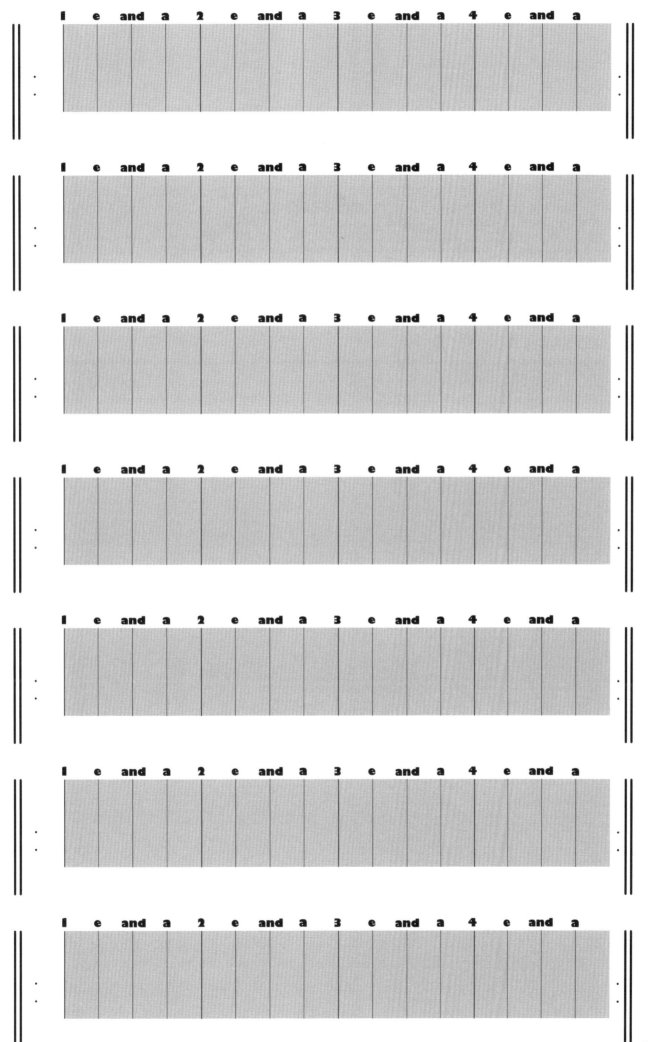

...The end of the workshop!

THE BEATLIFE BOOK